An Attic Full of Poems

An Attic Full of Poems

Best wishes,
Birdie Stringfellow

Birdie D. Stringfellow

Copyright © 2009 by Birdie D. Stringfellow.

Library of Congress Control Number: 2009905423
ISBN: Hardcover   978-1-4415-4215-1
                Softcover   978-1-4415-4214-4

All rights reserved. No part of this book may be reproduced or transmitted in any form or by any means, electronic or mechanical, including photocopying, recording, or by any information storage and retrieval system, without permission in writing from the copyright owner.

This book was printed in the United States of America.

To order additional copies of this book, contact:
Xlibris Corporation
1-888-795-4274
www.Xlibris.com
Orders@Xlibris.com

CONTENTS

Acknowledgments 9

An Old Lady Speaks 11
I Swallowed My Pen 13
The Caller 15
The Lake of Hope 16
Dictionary 17
The Fly 19
Avoiding Love 20
Smothered 21
Want a Drink? 23
Bars 25
A Desire for Solitude 27
The Joining 28
Dying? 29
I Took My Cat to the Dentist 30
Eddie 31
Friends 33
Like Jesus 34
The Milkman 35
You Melt My Heart 37
The Open Window 39
Watching You Sleep 40
Lottery Blues 41
The Unhappy Bird 43
Word 45
Humpty Dumpty Had a Great Fall 46
A Lady's Prayer 47
No Poem Today 48
Ten Minutes 49
Sentence 53

Death Does Not Come	55
The Ambush	57
Mind Flip	58
Stretched	59
My Very Best Friend	60
Sister, You're Beautiful	61
Warning	62
The Stick Fish	63
The Order of Things	65

Dedication

This book, An Attic Full of Poems, is dedicated to
my mother,
Ethelyn Lindsey Stringfellow.

Without her encouragement,
this book would not have been possible.

Acknowledgments

I give eminent thanks to the following people
who have inspired and advised me
throughout my writing life:
Ethelyn Lindsey Stringfellow,
Gale Stringfellow McCain
and
Lucile Barbre McLeroy.

I give gracious thanks
to my dearest friend,
Hina Vyas,
for always being there
to listen to me try-out
my newly written poems.

I thank Judith E. Jordan,
my special friend,
for the use of
her lovely photograph
on my book cover.

I also thank Leah Allison Fuqua
for all her magnificent posing
and the magic
she gave to my book.

I am thankful to Marilyn Meadows,
owner of ALIBI in Athens, Georgia,
for her photographic contribution
to my poem, "Bars."

I also thank Edwin Fuqua,
the best photographer I have ever met,
for capturing
the images in my book.

An Old Lady Speaks

Alright, nurses. Take a close look at me.
Things aren't always as they appear to be.
You think I'm testy. You think I'm mean.
But things aren't always as they seem to be.

You have a job to do all through the day.
You bathe and feed me and with my feelings, play.
You want that paycheck. That sums it up.
But you don't care about me—not very much.

I once was like you—young and carefree.
I had a husband and children numbering three.
I had a life. I was beautiful and smart.
I lived in a world in which I played a part.

Then I grew old like you will one day, too.
I could no longer put on my socks or my shoes.
I had to hire someone to look after me.
So here you are and here you will be

until my watch stops and my bell quits ringing.
The clouds will come up and the birds will cease singing.
My grass will dry up and my flowers will die.
The weeds will take over and destroy all life.

And you will move on and you will forget my face.
My name will fade away and another take its place.
You will have someone else to care for everyday,
but please be careful what you do and what you say

because she'll hear you and she'll know she's trouble.
She'll be cooperative and so very humble.
Don't play with her heart—it is ever so weak.
She wouldn't hurt a fly. She's really quite meek.

Please let her ride out her last days at a walk,
and when you address her, don't yell—just talk.
She doesn't want to be here anymore than you.
If only she could still put on her own shoes.

I Swallowed My Pen

I swallowed my pen on purpose.
I crammed it into my mouth,
chewed it up and gulped it down.

I was curious about how
words tasted so I ate my pen.
I followed it with water.

It wasn't bad at all.
It digested rather easily.
Words spread throughout my body

and ran through my veins.
My mind was consumed with them.
Thoughts and ideas developed quickly.

I began to write them down.
I chose my words carefully.
A poem was magically created.

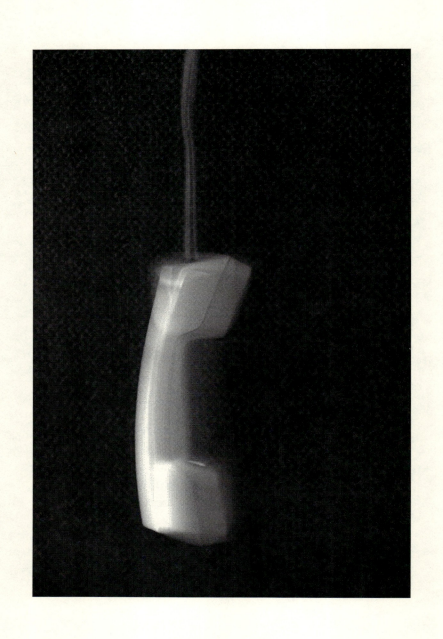

The Caller

He drove me crazy
with his constant phone calls.
At first, it was flattering.
As time wore on,
I could get no sleep.
My dreams consisted of telephone rings,
although they were not always in my imagination.
So I changed my number.
Somehow, he found it,
and the calls continued.

He started dropping by unannounced.
I moved and thus, changed my address.
He discovered that, also,
so there was only one thing left to do
to stop this nonsense.
I married him.

The phone calls stopped.
He quit popping over.
He left me . . .

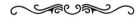

The Lake of Hope

My love for you
is melting
like the snow
dripping off the bush
outside of my window.

A lifetime of memories
has been branded
into my soul
like the iron
etched on a bull
staking a claim.

Only this ownership
is over with,
finished and
never to return.

The line has been cast
and this fish
is not biting.
The bait slowly
loosens from the hook
and wiggles quickly
for a moment,
then drowns.

This fish escapes
with her life
swimming freely
forevermore
in a lake of hope.

Dictionary

I am dictionary

I give meaning to the word
and individualize it

I arrange the word with
other words and give
new significance to it

I am King of the Words
and I rule over
my pages

I am the keeper
of the letters

The letters adhere
to the words
which adhere to the pages
which adhere to me

I form the meanings

I am dictionary

The Fly

The fly was sly—
not more than I.
He buzzed my head.
I wished him dead.

I chased him fast
until at last,
he landed hard
upon the bar.

I grabbed a swatter.
It did not matter.
My arm flew down.
He hit the ground.

I hit him again.
It was his end.
But as I crouched,
I heard an "ouch!"

Avoiding Love

To prevent myself from tasting love,
I stuff my mouth with food.
And because I stay away from love,
I'm in a better mood.

Smothered

Smothered by your love,
your attention,
your very presence—
I need space.

I am a shuttle
longing to soar
far away from
this place.

I am a neck
with a rope
tied around it
that is

pulling me
towards you
and against
my will.

I am a pillow
wrapped in plastic
with a warning
on its label.

I am drowning
in your love,
and you know
I cannot swim.

You won't let go,
but you must.

What I am is smothered.

I am suffocating now.
I have taken my last breath.
I am finished.

Want a Drink?

Years ago,
my mother
was undergoing
physical therapy
for an illness
called "neuropathy."
This refers to
a nerve disorder
of the legs
which prevents
the person
from walking
without assistance.

Mom was being
instructed on
how to use a
walker to combat
this condition,
and she was
extremely tired
and worn-out.
Sweat was just
pouring down
her little face.

The therapist
noticed this
and asked
my mother if
she would like
something to drink.
Shocked, my mother
replied, no thanks —
my doctor has
forbidden me to
mix alcohol with
the medicine
I am taking.

Will she
ever stop?!

Bars

He went to bars.

He drank at bars.

He got into fights
at bars.

He ended up
behind bars.

A Desire for Solitude

I demand some time alone

Manipulating people
are crowding me

I am badgered by others
imposing upon me

People I know
are stretching me thin
in all directions
so that I may split apart

My mind is spinning
and my insides are churning
from too much pressure
and jealousy from outside

I am living a struggle
not to jerk the phone
from the outlet plugged
securely into the wall

I am fighting a battle
not to rip the doorbell
from its resting spot beyond
this unreceptive home

I desire empty space
so that I may replenish it
with happiness and joy
and regain my own freedom

I demand some time alone

The Joining

I wake up with you next to me in our bed.
When I gaze upon you, I realize that you are dead.
My ancient one, breath has left your lips forever.
I never would have dreamed you'd leave me—never!
But we are old, collectible antiques on a shelf,
I have often thought hard when staring at myself:
our time on earth can't last—one day it'll disappear.
And now you, my love, have awakened all my fears.

What shall I do? Just lie here for a while?
And then I notice upon your face, there is a smile.
I long to share this joy you must have found.
My life won't be the same with you not around.
A tear leaves my eye and rolls down my face.
I wrap my arms around you for one final embrace.
I grab the bottle of pills beside our bed.
I take them all. Soon, too, I will be dead.

Dying?

Open Thou hand, my Lord,
that I may step into Thy palm.
A radiant, white light engulfs me—
I feel an everlasting calm.

The doctors all said I would go now,
but You had the final say.
Open Thou hand, my Lord,
so that I may find my way.

Your mercy endureth forever,
of that I am surely sure.
As I step up upon Your kindness,
I thank You, my precious Sir.

I feel the curl of Your fingers
as You kindly take me in.
You wrap Your hand around me
and forgive me all my sins.

We move up to the Heavens.
My soul is filled with love.
There is no such thing as dying
to the ones who live above.

I Took My Cat to the Dentist

I took my cat to the dentist
because at night he was keeping me awake.
It turns out he had TMJ
and a cat splint the dentist had to make.

That awful sounding grinding noise
my cat would make every time he slept
was chipping his teeth into pieces
and would always give me a headache.

But now that he has his splint,
he sleeps pretty well at that.
So do I; I have TMJ, too.
The silence—me and my cat.

Eddie

Eddie, you're more than a brother-in-law;
you're more like a brother to me.
You're always there to change the bulbs
when they go out and I can't see.

I'm not just talking about the bulbs in the house
but the bulbs that are within my heart.
And you have the twist that turns them on
when my world is falling apart.

When my sister's not around and I'm in a fix,
it's you who comes running to help.
I thank you for coming with a smile on your face,
creating memories that will always be kept.

Friends

Friends are hard to come by
of the lasting kind.
But then I found that's not true
once upon a time.

Your kindness and understanding
calmed all my fears inside,
and the closeness we felt for each other
took sprout, and you did hide

my secrets and my worries.
You told me not to fret.
You wouldn't tell a single soul.
My secrets would be kept.

We've only become closer
throughout the time we've known
each other, and we do things
like go out and chat on the phone.

I can tell already this much—
our friendship will never end.
I'm so very glad I met you.
You'll always be my friend!

Like Jesus

She grabbed the hen
around the neck
and crucified her.

The Milkman

Mama, why are you crying? Is there no milk for our cereal this morning? What happened to the milkman? He always comes and delivers his goods by now. I don't mind eating my cereal dry! I like my food crunchy. Sometimes the milk makes my breakfast soggy. Did you know that? Mama, please don't cry!

Mama, why do people say I favor the milkman? What on earth do they mean? Am I not as nice to the postman as I am to the milkman?

You Melt My Heart

You melt my heart
like the sun
melts the snow
after a winter storm.

You touch my mind
like a pianist
touches the keys
on her beloved piano.

You grab my soul
like a baby
grabs his blanket
to keep him warm.

You stir my senses
like a chef
stirs a kettle
of porridge, delicately.

You make me
the person
I truly am.

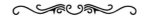

The Open Window

I was writing a poem
the other day
when it slipped out
of the window.
I tried to shut it in,
but it was
too late to catch it,
and it blew away.

The poem rode out
on a breeze
and was gone quickly
from my view.
I opened the window
and called it
by name though received
no answer.

Another day would come;
it would return.
I held my pen in hand
and waited,
although the moment
had passed me by.
There would be no poem.
Some other time perhaps.

Watching You Sleep

You are sleeping
I'm watching you
Handsome face
Eyes so blue
Sensuous ears
Beautiful smile
Let me stay
And watch awhile

Lottery Blues

I win what I spend
and I spend what I win.
I guess you could call
that breaking even.

The Unhappy Bird

Let me out! Please let me out!
the caged bird begins to cry.
If I stay in here much longer,
I know that I will surely die!

Let me out! Please let me out!
the caged bird begins to scream.
Oh why can't this just be
some horrible, horrible dream?!

You watch him flap and flap and flap
his beautiful, yellow wings.
You think—oh, what a happy bird,
this grand, delightful thing.

But the bird is thinking differently.
He feels like he's in jail.
He wants to be out with his friends.
Like a ship, he wants to sail.

A tear trickles from his pretty eye,
and you begin to fret.
You think he's sick and worry hard,
and then you call your vet.

You drive your bird to see his 'doc'.
He gives him meds to take.
He tells you to quit worrying.
He'll get better for goodness sakes.

The poor caged bird is still crying.
He thinks, they'll never understand.
I don't belong within these bars—
I belong outside upon the land.

His wings he goes to flapping—
another bruise beneath his breast.
He begins to sing and call for rescue
to his family outdoors within their nest.

The young owner thinks he's well.
The young owner is oh-so wrong.
He has misinterpreted the flapping.
He has misinterpreted the song.

Depression has taken over.
The bird's mind is one big fog.
He drops dead upon the cage floor.
A bird ain't nothing like a dog.

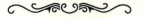

Word

My name is Word.

My cousins are many.

It is I who adds meaning to your moods.

It is I who makes your existence possible.

Without me, you are nothing.

A book without its pages.

I drink ink and eat paper.

I define knowledge.

I reek of wisdom.

I am Word.

I form the sentence which gives meaning to your life.

I am the reason you are able to read this right now.

I am Word.

Rest in me and exist!

Humpty Dumpty Had a Great Fall

Humpty Dumpty had a great fall,
so he couldn't attend the President's ball.
When told of this news,
he started to ramble,
so the CIA said
he'd be better off
scrambled.

A Lady's Prayer

Let my life show purpose and deed.
Let my belly give breath to seed.
Let my days not be numbered but sane.
Let me not have lived my life in vain.

No Poem Today

The mockingbird startled me while I tried to write a poem. I became lost and my brain quit churning like butter gone sour. All thoughts slipped away and neurons collided like ships crashing into icebergs.

The mockingbird laughed at me. I did not laugh back. The poem was destroyed and I cried for its return.

I heard the screaming in my head. If not for that, I would have thought I was dead. But poems do not die. This one would be back, safely tucked away in my gray matter for now, after the flying creature had departed. I would have to wait. No poem today.

Ten Minutes

I was on the phone!

Who with? Some guy?!

No, a girl friend of mine.
Don't worry about it.

Yeah, I bet you were!
Don't lie to me. Tell me.
Who were you talking with?!

I told you. Just a friend.

I don't believe you, liar.
You're going to get caught.
There will be hell to pay.
You know that, don't you?

An ache was planted in her head.
Unplugging herself from the tension,
she immaculated her home.
She left nothing untouched

just as he had not left her untouched.
Bruises covered her skin and mind.
A relationship of broken bones,
broken words and a broken heart.

She began mopping floors
and dusting all of the furniture.
She gathered up the laundry
and threw it in the washer.

She wiped down her glass back door
so that it was reflection-free
and gave off an invisible hue,
hidden to the human eye.

She thought about all the times
he had hurt her, by the hand
as well as by the tongue.
And she hated him.

The phone rang and she answered.

Who's over there with you?

No one. I am all alone.

You're lying to me. Who is he?

I'm telling you the truth, honey.
Nobody is here but me, honest.

I don't believe you. You're lying again.
I'm coming over. Don't lie to me!

Oh, no, she thought. Another beating.
She scrubbed even harder
until her bathtub glistened.
Her heart was pounding with fear.

She couldn't get away from him.
She had tried to before. Big mistake.
He always found her, always.
It wasn't very pleasant when he did.

Now he was coming over
because he thought she had company.
She heard a crash and glass breaking.
She ran to see what had happened.

He had walked straight through
the transparent glass door,
thinking it was wide open,
because it was so shiny and clean.

He had cut himself badly.
There was a bloody mess everywhere.
He was down on the floor
begging for her to help him.

Ah, baby, please help me.
I am bleeding to death.
I think I might be dying.
Baby, baby, please help me.

She looked at him with no passion
in her hollow brown eyes.
She reached for the phone,
then had second thoughts.

She replaced the rescue phone
back on its cradle and
she sat in her favorite chair.
How long would this take?

Ten minutes? Not any longer.
Yes, that sounded about right.

Ah, baby, please help me.
I'm hurt bad. I can't move. Help me.

She glanced at her Timex.
Ten minutes. She waited.
She checked her watch again.
Five more minutes.

He wasn't speaking anymore.
He wasn't moving either.
She got up from her chair
and approached him.

She tapped him with her foot.
He didn't move. Good.
No response. Heavy, too.
She looked at her Timex again.

Time's up. Ten minutes was up.
She reached for the phone
and began to dial.

Nine-one-one? This is an emergency!

Sentence

Sentence is my name.

I give emphasis
to the words.

Without me,
limitations and boundaries
gain control of the mind.

Knowledge is wiped out
and ignorance is
all-consuming.

I am relied upon
for the expression
of feelings.

I am relied upon
for providing
definitions.

I am relied upon
for recording
thoughts and
ideas.

Without me,
there would
be no language.

I am sentence.

Death Does Not Come

Others wait in another dimension
coaxing the soon-to-be departed
to take a step over.

Death growls wildly
for the capture
of its prey.

However, they are not listening.
Hands are cupped
over their ears.

Clouds of fear settle over the sky.
A barrier is laid out, and
nothing can break through.

But it is time.
Where is the rattle?

The Ambush

When I was a walking toddler,
I use to ambush my parents
in their bed
every night.

I couldn't understand why my dad
would become so irate with me,
sending me back
to my own bed.

I would actually lift up their covers
and crawl under the sheets, placing myself
right in the center of
their two naked bodies.

Now that I am older,
I believe I understand
the bare facts
of this matter.

Mind Flip

He flipped her mind over and over again
like a fried egg being heated mercilessly
until the edges curled back,
and she broke apart.

Sections could no longer be pieced back together.
A scrambled puzzle lay waiting to be deciphered.
She became ignorant
of her own needs.

She judged herself harshly for letting this happen.
Her shell had been cracked and could not be reversed.
She became his meal,
and he feasted on her.

She was no longer his piece de resistance.
He had consumed all of her, body and mind.
Used up, she was.
He soon spat her out.

A lesson to be learned is a reward to be gained.
Do not stray too close to the fire, or you might get burned.
Respect yourself,
and respect will be yours.

Stretched

I am a rubberband
being stretched too thin
from both ends

I am a yawn
being stretched too wide
at the jaws

I am two arms
being stretched too high
in the air

I hurt all over
The pain is unbearable
I ache

This rubberband has popped
This yawn has locked-up
These arms have broken

I have lost my elasticity
I have lost my freedom
I have lost my power to heal

I am stretched
too thin,
too wide
and too high

I need
some
distance

My Very Best Friend

You're the very best friend I've ever had.
When I'm with you, I'm never sad.
I'm middle-aged now. My hair's turning gray.
Although when we get together, we laugh and play

like when I was a young kid growing up
and knowing the meaning of "living it up!"
We have such fun. We're sneaky, too,
like telling fibs about the things we do.

It's a wonder we haven't spent a night in jail
or received a ticket in the mail.
When I'm with you, I'm so happy and glad.
You're the very best friend I've ever had.

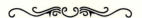

Sister, You're Beautiful

Sister, you're beautiful.
Look what you've done.
You've brought the goodness
and the sun

into my life
without even trying.
I remember the days
when I was crying,

and you would hug me
and squeeze me tight.
You turned my darkness
into light.

I'd be distressed
about who knows what,
and there you'd be
with your sisterly touch.

You calmed my fears
so many times.
I love you, Sister,
and I'm glad you're mine.

Warning

Psalms 23 is a favorite

to all who know God's Word.

Never take the Lord's name in vain.

There are those who haven't heard.

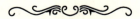

The Stick Fish

She had never fished before, but she wanted to learn how. He took her to his lake house where he promised she would get the chance.

He grabbed a plain old pole, baited it with a red worm and threw the line in the water. They waited five minutes. Then five minutes more.

The wind blew. The line tugged, and the pole pulled slightly in her hands. The line tugged some more.

"You've got a bite," he yelled. "Jerk the rod quickly, upward, and hook him!"

She did as she was told. She grabbed the line with one hand, held the pole with the other and pulled the stick in.

The Order of Things

I reached towards the sky
I grabbed hold of a cloud,
so light, it blew out of my hand
I tried to catch it
and succeeded for one moment
although it melted in my hand like
a piece of cotton candy
and was gone

I reached towards the sky
I grabbed hold of the sun,
so hot, it burned my hand,
and I pushed it away
The palm of my hand
beheld its image
in my own self-made tattoo
I could see my reflection
within, and I liked it

I reached towards the sky
although this time the sky
slapped my hand away
and pleaded with me
to leave it untouched
as it was meant to be,
so I did

I looked around me,
and I saw the earth
It was ready for me,
so I bent down
and picked the most
beautiful flower
I have ever seen

Then the flower
spoke to me
Please leave me be
I belong in this soil
where I will grow
and start a family
Never had I looked
at a flower in that way,
so I replanted it
The flower smiled at me,
and I smiled back

Now every time I look
at the sky above
or the earth below
I see a different view
of the world itself
I am in the middle
I admire this order
of the way things are
Never again will I
try to rearrange
what has been so
perfectly created

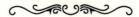

Get Published, Inc!
Thorofare, NJ 08086
04 September 2009
BA2009247